Paradise Place

ANDERSON DOVILAS

CMS
BOOK PUBLISHING

ISBN-13:
978-0692883280

ISBN-10:
0692883282

DEDICATION

I wrote this book for the tears that roll down our cheeks, which we
are quick to wipe away and forget, and thus we are quick to miss
the joy hidden beneath each drop.
I don't know exactly how you will grow after reading this collection
of thoughts, but I do know your heart will grow heavy at times.
Whenever you feel like the reading is too hard on your soul, simply
turn the page... hope is always on the other side.

Anderson DOVILAS

CONTENTS

ACKNOWLEDGMENTS

Special thanks to those who let me borrow their words to write this book, and to those who shared sleepless nights with me while navigating grammar and other figures of speech to shape this work.

I also express my gratitude to Lynn Williams for the editing. Your final touch filtered the sentences until they were ready to be easily enjoyed.

Foreword

As the mother of one, soon to be two, young boys, the world has become a somewhat darker place. The need to protect my children from the ills in this world has given me such anxiety as I'd never before felt it was possible to feel. Compound this with the desire and need to make sure my sons learn the hardest lessons of life, while experiencing as little damage as possible, in order to grow into good men, and parenting is a daunting task indeed.

It is unfortunate that many in this world who have children simply are not up to the task. Yet I like to believe in my heart that most people are, and though everyone makes mistakes, we love our children and want the best for them. When we can't provide the best of some things, we try to compensate in other areas. Sadly, this can lead to disastrous results. For example, a lack of loving attention and compassion cannot be replaced by material goods, or a fine education, or anything else that money can possibly buy. Trauma cannot be erased by luxury.

My own childhood was relatively happy, but as an adult and now a parent I can better appreciate the tougher

times. I was raised by a single mother and I had two younger half-brothers. Growing up without either of the men who were supposed to be my father-figures gave me a great sadness, yet now I see that though my insecurities stemming from that were inevitable, I can also see that I may have turned out much worse if they'd been present. At times, both tried to buy my affection and forgiveness, only to disappear again without warning.

My mother tried her very best to give us all of the love and attention we deserved as children, and sacrificed a great deal. She made a small income in childhood education so that she could be with us every moment that we weren't at school, even summer time. We lived with her mother, and their relationship was tumultuous... another sacrifice she made so that we could have a decent home. Of course there were times when we rebelled. I had my moments that shattered her world; we all watched helplessly as my brother descended into drug abuse; my other brother struggled mightily with his own demons. A family member's suicide created an enormous rift that still hasn't quite healed.

Recalling these harrowing experiences that *still* happened despite a moderately privileged upbringing makes me toss and turn at night, wondering how in the

world I can possibly mitigate the coming difficulties I will be facing as a mother myself.

When I read the short stories that make up *Paradise Place*, I was further absorbed into my fears and anxieties about my young family. These coming-of-age tales bring to light the moments in childhood that so many experience but few are brave enough to talk about. The loss of one's innocence to the world's cruelty, the awakening of compassion through sacrifice, and the discovery that even the friendliest of faces can be that of a dangerous predator; all of these moments are experienced by everyone in some form or another.

Us parents cannot possibly protect our children from these experiences, and yet we try. These stories demonstrate at times that even such a well-meaning endeavor can blow up in our faces. I can vouch for their authenticity, because I watched my own mother experience it several times between the three of us. Sometimes we start to believe in the utopia we have created in our children's minds, and we panic when they inform us that the fantasy has already been shattered when we weren't paying close enough attention. Other times, we continue to hold our heads down in the sand and pretend that this imaginary paradise is still real, rather than face the truth and what it

means for a growing child.

Anderson Dovilas' *Paradise Place* showed me, and at times reminded me, through stories written thoughtfully and with raw emotion, that even the most golden of childhoods can be marred by a single tragedy; that even the most loving of parents can fail their babies; and that even our most trusted friends can be the greatest dangers to our children.

However, I also saw that even the most heinous acts can be recovered from; that disaster can lead to unity; and that ultimately, our children will come to a crossroads at several points in life and just *maybe*, with the proper guidance, they will choose the correct path.

Though it is every parent's hope that *their* guidance and *their* wisdom will be what steers the course, we must accept that we are still human, and we are each flawed in many ways. The proper path for us is not necessarily the proper path for another person, even our own children. Other people are placed into our lives and into our children's lives, and even adults need the benefits from these shared experiences.

The most important lessons that I think can be gathered from these stories is that children *must* be protected, but not from the things we think. Of course the

obvious: sexual predators, drug traffickers, violence, etc. However, and most terrifying of all, they must be protected at times from *us*, their own parents, even the most doting among us. Too many times, children are dismissed when telling a painful truth, a truth that can be so terrible that it kills us to imagine that it might be true. We flare up, call them liars, tell them that they're exaggerating, and maybe even punish them for daring to seek help. Sometimes, the biggest obstacle to a child's well-being is the person or people who love them the most.

With that, I present to you *Paradise Place*. In its entirety, this heavy work is both a beacon of hope for the times of trial and a cautionary tale for anyone who thinks they can wrestle their children through a perfect childhood.

~ **Lynn Williams**
March 28th, 2017

ANDERSON DOVILAS

PARADISE PLACE

My earliest recollections of my childhood were the sweet memories at Paradise Place. The name really suited it. I remember playing in the park after school with other children. I remember the tea parties, slumber parties, movie nights, and the abundance of food. I remember the pool. Every Sunday was always fun. It was like a big family at Paradise Place; skin color or race did not matter. Neither did religion. And there was Julio, my best friend. Like mine, his family was also migrants. I cannot remember how we became friends, but I remembered that he was always my partner.

I remember the holidays, Christmas especially, because of the anticipation of our special Christmas party. Christmas was always full of gifts, full of games to play, full of hugs from family, cousins, and little cousins. I also recall the great big pool where we all played and splashed on Sundays. Like Dad says, "Those were times when we and our friends did not need alcohol to have fun." With a touch of nostalgia in my voice, I was describing those Sundays of fun to my teacher and said, "Sunday was the loudest day at the swimming pool; my dad even said,

'Adults don't need alcohol to blend themselves in the party.' The little girls sit on their fathers' knees playing with their beards, and the little boys with small arms protect their moms from the waves."

I recall that I never saw a gate. Dad says we didn't need gates for security. The natural harmonization of the parents and the joyful days of the children after school made the place happy and peaceful. What we had was better than the most secure systems.

What I loved best about Paradise Park was my daily ritual with Julio. Every evening, we used to run around trying to find the sun as it set. Everything was a game to us. Oh! How we had lots of fun! There were times when we would lie down on the grass at night with my dad. Whenever we went for our nightly stroll, I discovered the beauty of the moon as it played hide and seek with the clouds. I used to imagine Julio and I were the moon and the other children were our playmates. Oftentimes, whenever Julio joined my dad and me, we would point out different shapes and figures amidst the clouds.

Sometimes I wondered if I dreamed it all up, because the happiness, peace, and comfort I felt in Paradise Place was something worthy of fantasy. Other times, when I think of how I used to feel so secure and happy back then,

I ask myself is it because of the innocence of my childhood? I wish I could go back to that phase, but it is a little too late.

***

"Daddy!" I screamed as I ran to the door to welcome him. It was movie night in our complex and my dad was to get the corn seeds for the popcorn. I was so excited because we were about to watch a new movie. Julio was excited because Daddy had promised that he would allow us make the popcorn with his supervision if we were on our best behavior. We were restless in class that day and even our teacher, Miss Nicole, noticed it. At dinner, I wolfed down my food so that Mommy would not complain. I also did my homework and had my bath without being told. It seemed like time was moving slowly all day. I even cleaned my room and helped Mommy with the dishes.

In preparation for the movie, the boys were helping the men arrange the chairs and set up the screen. Julio and I helped Daddy get the popcorn machine ready. As soon as the corn started popping, we started singing our popcorn song which we had learned watching Barney, our favorite show. We helped Daddy distribute popcorn bowls to everyone. We felt proud because it was a lot of responsibility we had been given. At seven o'clock,

everyone had settled in their chairs with a bowl of popcorn and a glass of lemonade made available by Mr. Joseph and his wife, the apartment managers.

Julio, my favorite buddy, sat beside me as usual. During the movie, Julio and I took a pinky swear to attend the same college. In our world, everything was perfect. Little did we know that life as we knew it was about to change.

***

It was my turn to hold our monthly slumber party, and we were all huddled in the sitting room watching our favorite cartoon: Snow White and the Seven Dwarfs. There were eight children in our complex within my age group. Usually when we watched Snow White we did a role play of characters in it. But on this day Pearl, Mr. Joseph's daughter, was sad. In our bid to make her happy we allowed her to play the role of Snow White, but she was still not cheerful. So we started singing the nursery rhyme, "Oh dear why are you crying?" Halfway through the song, she burst into tears and said, "My daddy says we are leaving Paradise Park. I heard him telling Mommy this afternoon. I don't want to go... no more slumber parties," she sobbed, "no more pool Sundays, no more movie nights."

We were all shocked because for as long as we could remember, no family had moved out of Paradise Park. We didn't understand the full import of it, but we all gave her a group hug and promised that we would always invite her for the parties and her parents could drive down to Paradise Park for our usual pool Sundays.

The following morning, at the breakfast table, I told my parents what Pearl had said. They were surprised that the Josephs were moving out and didn't inform anybody. My mommy said, "Surely they owe it to us to give prior notice if they are leaving."

Daddy said, "This is beyond the usual manager/tenant relationship. I thought we were family." It was obvious my parents were lost in thought about this development.

I left for school with the other children, but Pearl did not go with us. We were sad because apart from a few times when one of us was sick, there was never a time we did not go to school together. In fact in school, our teacher, Miss Nicole, had given us the name "Paradise team."

After school, while we were playing in the park, we saw a man come out from Mr. Joseph's office with a pile of papers under his arm. He set out, pasting some of the papers on the notice board; the others he tucked into the

doors of each apartment. As soon as he was done, he walked towards us with a look of scorn and said, "Sunny days are over, kids," and walked away. We took little notice of him and soon continued playing.

Mr. Joseph called for an apartment meeting that evening. It was there he that broke the news that he and his family were moving out and that his replacement was moving in the next day. The memos that had been given to each apartment showed that the management company had been changed, and the new company wanted to make structural changes to the complex. The other kids and I wished for a bigger park, or a bigger pool, or a lake with ducks in it. But the adults were a little skeptical, and hoped that this new company was going to take everyone into consideration when making the adjustments.

There was a sort of sadness in the air. There was an impromptu send-off party, but it was not as lively as our usual parties were.

***

After the Josephs had moved out, we were expecting our new manager to have a family too. But to our shock, our new manager, Mr. Smith, was a middle-aged man who smelled of cigarettes. He never smiled. When he first arrived, we threw him a welcome party which he did

not attend. He had said, "Parties are waste of time." On the playground, whenever we saw him coming, we cringed because he was bound to scold us for no reason. He also cursed a lot. Things were no longer the same; little did we know, the worst was yet to come.

Shortly after Mr. Smith moved in, there was a complex meeting. After the meeting, I could tell that my parents were not happy. I heard my mom tell Dad that we should start looking for a new home because Paradise Place was no longer going to be like the paradise we used to know.

The next day, while we were leaving for school, some trucks came into our complex. They brought different machinery. Cody, who hardly talked, told us that his mom and dad had mentioned that there wasn't going to be any more pool. We all cried out in outrage, but we hoped that deep down, Cody got it all wrong. Unfortunately, by the time we got back from school, our once beautiful pool was half-gone. A few weeks later, the park was also cleared to make room for another building. They soon erected security gates and a new set of rules, such as no partying. Kids were no longer allowed to play around. Pets were also not allowed.

***

That year, Christmas came without its usual good mood. This was because most of our neighbors were moving out. Even Julio! The new management company had increased the rent and also changed conditions. People without a resident permit could not stay. Unfortunately, Julio's family was not able to secure their resident permit. Most of the other families decided that they could not pay the higher rent. Mommy and Daddy argued constantly on whether or not to move out. I was just sad that Julio was leaving.

After the other families began moving out, new families moved in. I had mixed feelings. I wanted to make new friends but I missed my old friends, especially Julio. The new building was completed. I did not like the idea of seeing a new building instead of the park from my bedroom window. Before the end of the year, a family had moved into one of the new apartments, apartment 108. From my bedroom window, I could see into one of the rooms. I secretly hoped that the new family had a child my age, and that room would be his or her room so that when we became friends, we could see each other from our windows. My wish was partly granted. The family had a little boy, but he was younger. I did not mind. I was desperate for a new friend.

The day after they moved in, I dragged my dad to go welcome them since we were the only neighbors they had for now. Mommy baked a pie which we brought along. We pressed the bell and a big burly man opened the door. He was nothing like we expected. We introduced ourselves as the neighbors. He did not ask us to come in. He only asked, "Whaddya want?" We showed him the pie as a welcome gift, but his only reply was, "I don't need nosy neighbors in my f**king business. Stay out of my business, and I'll stay out of yours." With that, he slammed the door in our faces.

I was shocked because I had never seen anyone apart from Mr. Smith curse, and no one was ever rude. My parents were embarrassed. We sat down and ate our pie. My dad warned me never to go up to apartment 108 again.

***

Two weeks after the embarrassing incident, I was getting ready for bed when I heard screams from apartment 108. I heard the man curse loudly and say to the little boy that he was going to make sure each broken shard of glass cut him as his punishment for breaking a plate. The boy continued to scream and cry. I remembered the talk we had gotten about the essence of 911. I dialed the number and reported what I'd heard. I rushed to the living room to call

my babysitter, Chloe, as my parents were out. But by then, the screams had stopped. She felt I was imagining things. She read me to sleep and by the next day, I had forgotten all about the incident.

A few weeks later, while Daddy and I were going out to get groceries, we saw our neighbor in apartment 108 rush out with the boy in his arms towards the car. He was unconscious and was bleeding from the nose. He drove out in a hurry. My daddy tried to cover my eyes to prevent me from seeing such a horrible sight, but it was too late. On our way, I told him about what I'd heard on the night he and Mommy went out. He said I should not get involved and ignore it all.

Later that night, the complex was crawling with police officers and social workers. One of the police officers knocked on the door. He asked my parents if they had seen or heard anything unusual happening in apartment 108. My parents had not. They informed him that the man had expressly cautioned them not to get into his business. Dad also described the scene at the car park to him. My parents were then informed that the boy had died, and they were sad. They tried to explain death to me, but in my mind I saw it as a good thing. The boy had gone to rest in a better place. I didn't understand their sadness.

A few days later, another cop came around our apartment. Mom had gone to get groceries and Daddy was working on something on his laptop. I opened the door to him and he asked for my parents. I told him my daddy was busy and Mom wasn't around. He asked me if I knew what 911 was for and I proudly told him all I had learned about it in school. He asked if I had ever made a 911 call and I told him of the incident. While we were talking, my daddy came in and saw me talking to the cop. He was furious. The policeman, sensing my dad's anger, explained to him that I had been helpful to their case. Investigation had shown that the boy was severely abused. He also told him that I had made a 911 call once before. He thanked me, apologized to my dad, and took his leave.

After the policeman left, Daddy asked why I didn't tell him about the call. I told him I tried to tell him but he would not listen. He said nothing about it and I kept quiet. I was scared that he was going to hit me for doing something like that.

Things were so different from how they used to be. My parents argued more often about moving out, and I was scared. I felt like Daddy was changing. I started having nightmares about Daddy beating me, about Daddy carrying me to the hospital with blood all over my body. I became

withdrawn. I stayed in my room a lot. Later that week, a police officer came to inform my parents that they needed me to testify about what I had heard from apartment 108. My parents argued more about it.

A few days later in school, I realized I did not do my homework. When Miss Nicole tried to ask why I didn't do it, my stomach hurt. My mouth was dry. I felt this urge to run away from all of them. I felt like Miss Nicole was going to hit me. I watched her move closer. As she reached out to touch me, I suddenly pushed my way past her and ran. I ran out of the class into an empty toilet stall. The school counselor came to talk me into returning to class. I stopped paying attention in class, stopped doing assignments. Soon I was suspended and Miss Nicole had to call a parent-teacher meeting. My parents were surprised. She told them about everything that had been going on with me at school. She was surprised they hadn't noticed and told them they needed to pay more attention to me.

That evening, my parents called me into their room. I was expecting my daddy to hit me or even shout at me. I started freaking out. I was hyperventilating so they had to rush me to the hospital. I had a panic attack. My parents decided it was time for us to move.

A week later, we moved out and I got a therapist. It

took me a long while to let go of my fears. Though things are not as good as they were at Paradise Place, they are definitely better than what they'd become.

ANDERSON DOVILAS

SEPARATE PATH

Fredrick White was waiting for his four o'clock appointment. For the first time, he was quite nervous about seeing this patient. In all his years of practicing as a psychologist, he had not encountered this kind of case. He made himself a cup of coffee and tried to relax. Just as the coffee was ready, his secretary buzzed

"Doctor, your four o'clock is here," she said.

"Okay Brenda send him right in," he replied.

Though he did not think he was ready, he knew he had to face this demon.

Fredrick watched as the boy walked into his office. The expression on his face was sour. Obviously, no 16-year-old kid liked going to see a "shrink." The boy sat without being asked and regarded Fredrick with resentment. Fredrick observed his demeanor and felt the urge to help him.

Derek was sour. How could his parents do this to him? *I am never going to forgive them*, he thought. He watched the shrink he had been sent to. He realized the guy was a lot younger than he expected. *At least he dresses well*, he thought.

After about five minutes of silence, during which

both of them regarded each other, Fredrick broke the silence. "Lemonade or soda?" he asked.

"Um..soda," Derek said, suddenly feeling thirsty.

"Get it from the fridge," replied Fredrick.

As Derek walked towards the fridge, he saw different Lakers stickers and souvenirs on a shelf. Fredrick had learned from Derek's file that he was the star of his high school's basketball team. Being a big Lakers fan himself, he had decided the sport was going to be an ice breaker. Seeing that the display had produced its desired effect on Derek, he smiled to himself and felt more at ease.

"Lakers Gang, huh?" Derek couldn't stop himself from blurting out.

Fredrick smiled and replied, "All the time."

Immediately they both fell into a friendly banter about their favorite Lakers moments and stars.

"Do you intend to play professional basketball?"Fredrick asked.

Not expecting the question, Derek paused for a bit.

"I don't know, man. On the court is the only place I don't feel pressured or alone. It is the only place I feel free. I don't wanna jeopardize that by making it professional. I am afraid the thrill will just *pffft* into thin air."

"Take it easy, man. You don't have to decide now.

You still have your whole life ahead of you," Fredrick assured him.

"You really sure you're a shrink?"

"What do you mean?" asked Fredrick, a little confused.

"Um... I mean... I thought all shrinks were boring with a bad sense of humor. Erm... but you are different from my other shrinks. None of them dressed cool or discussed interesting things like basketball," Derek stammered.

"Gee... I guess that's a compliment. Thanks man," replied Fredrick, who was surprised by how quickly they had bonded.

"I gotta go now, I got practice and Coach would have my neck if I don't show up in time," said Derek, standing up to leave.

Fredrick nodded and was about to say something when Derek surprised him by inviting him to watch his next game later that week. Fredrick decided the only way he could really help the kid was to get closer and form a bond, so he agreed. As Derek stepped out of Fredrick's office, Fredrick wondered about the kind of pressure the teenager must be going through to push him to drugs.

He was soon lost in thought about his past. He

wondered what had become of his other friends, Patrick Duviver and Roberto Lopez. He was overwhelmed by a sense of gratitude that he had not ended up in the gutters.

***

Fredrick spotted Derek as soon as he took his seat on the bleachers by the court. The young man was making some awesome moves; he was better than Fredrick had thought.

Derek was about to give up on Fredrick showing up. He felt stupid for inviting his shrink in the first place. The guys would make fun of him if they found out he had to see a shrink in the first place. Oddly, he had wanted to impress Fredrick and he had found himself looking forward to the match not for the fun of it, but to have another time with Fredrick. He was starting to consider him as the elder brother he never had.

"Derek, boy, you're going soft," he muttered under his breath.

As soon as he saw Fredrick take his seat on the bleachers, his determination to win was doubled, and all the old thoughts disappeared. By the end of the game, his team had won with ninety-eight points to eighty-two. After the jubilation, he walked over to Fredrick.

"Thanks for coming, man. I didn't think you were

going to show up."

Fredrick was amused. He knew that from that statement, the young man had been let down a lot in the past. He simply smiled. They walked towards Fredrick's car, discussing the game.

"Did your parents make it for the game?" Fredrick asked.

"Nah...they have never seen me play."

Fredrick dropped the subject and they talked some more before he finally left. On his way home, Fredrick thought about the neglect that the young man was facing. He realized that their case was similar. He felt a tug towards Derek. He wanted to help him out. He was more than determined to help Derek make a meaningful life out of his existence.

***

It was Monday, one of the days Derek hated the most. Somehow, he found himself looking forward to it. He finally felt like he found someone who understood and was not judgmental. Being the star of his school's basketball team, he had no issues having people to hang out with, but they all expected him to be a jerk. His mom died when he was six months old so he never got to know her; his dad was never around either. He had grown up in the hands of

nannies and housekeepers.

When eventually his dad came around, he always forced him to go to the accounting firm because he wanted Derek to turn out like him and take over the firm after college. Derek shuddered as he conjured an image of himself wearing a suit and a tie, writing over ledgers, trying to balance accounts. His dad had no idea he even played basketball. Derek's dad hated basketball and considered it a sheer waste of time. Once Derek had heard him tell someone that basketball was for lazy men who ran around a court all day dunking balls into a basket.

His cell rang. As soon as he heard whose voice it was, he froze. Chas, his dealer... former dealer.

"How did you get my number?" he managed to say.

"Dee boy, you know me, I can get any and everything I want, I hear you clean now, good for you, boy. Trust me, you'll miss the old life soon."

Derek was dumbfounded. This same man had tried to ruin his life. He recalled how they'd met; it was at one of the celebratory parties. It had been at his buddy, Ben's house. He had tried a line of cocaine because the other guys were doing the same, but he'd almost choked. Chas had been there. The guys all made fun of him and Chas had promised to teach him how to snort it well. The next day,

Chas followed him home from school and this time around, he snorted two lines. He felt really good. Chas made a deal to supply him the substance regularly.

Before he knew it, he was hooked... until that fateful day, when he had nearly died from an overdose. That was when he was forced into rehab. Basketball was his only motivation to live. His dad had been to the hospital only once while he was there. Even after he came out of rehab, his dad had not been home.

***

By four o'clock, Fredrick was expecting Derek. He had something different planned. It was not going to be their usual office session. He was going to drive Derek to his roots, the ghetto, and tell his own story. It was a demon he had not confronted since he'd gotten out.

As soon as Derek arrived, they went for the drive. Fredrick took Derek to the place where he had lived as a kid.

"It's time I told you a story. My story actually," Fredrick began.

"I was 10 years old when my Dad left. My mom had no job, so she sold the house, set up a business, and moved into that building," he pointed to a tall building which looked deserted and about to crumble, "Not having

any experience in business, the business failed, so she had to get a job. She started working as a waitress but then the tips and her pay could not pay our bills, so she had to get a night job as a bartender in a bar. She couldn't afford a babysitter for me, so I was always home alone. Soon, I made friends with two boys in our building. Patrick and Roberto. They were migrants and like me, they were always home alone after school because their parents had to work two jobs to keep food on the table, and to keep the lights on. We became fast friends. We walked to school together, played basketball in our backyard. We used to fancy ourselves as part of the Lakers. Because we were poor, we could not join the basketball team in school. We simply could not afford it.

"By the time we turned fifteen, we hated our lives. Kids made fun of us and called us 'the rats.' We were miserable about it. One evening, while we were hanging out, bitching about life, Roberto and I started throwing stones. Unfortunately for us, one of the stones broke the windshield of an oncoming vehicle. The vehicle belonged to the Cold Beast, the notorious leader of one of the drug gangs in the area. We couldn't run because we knew he was going to find us anyway. So we stayed there, frozen, expecting the worst. The Cold Beast sent one of his men to

bring us to his den. We thought our lives were over and we would never come out alive.

"Luckily for us, the Cold Beast claimed to be in a good mood. He decided that we were going to work for him until our services could replace the windshield. We were happy at that prospect because it was better than death. We started off cleaning cars, shoes, and apartments of the gang members. Soon, the Cold Beast picked an interest in us and had us deliver packages to people. He bought us clothes and shoes, so we stopped looking like homeless kids. We had no trouble hiding all these from our parents because they were always busy. Little did we know that we had become drug traffickers. We only enjoyed the prestige of being seen with the Gang. Kids at school began to fear us. They no longer called us the rats. Neither did they play pranks on us. We felt on top of the world. We felt like men.

"On the eve of Roberto's 16th birthday, the Cold Beast made us take our first shot of heroin and told us we were officially part of the crew. That day, our innocence was taken from us. We drank and partied with the gang.

"We kept on delivering drugs for the gang, among other things. The Cold Beast particularly liked Patrick because of his innocent looks and charm.

"By the time we turned seventeen, we'd become

full-time dealers. We were also using drugs. Our parents believed that we'd found a job as delivery boys for a hardware store.

"Following a tip, there was a police raid on our base. The gang was not going down without a fight. Many of our members were killed, but the Cold Beast escaped. We were arrested. We were not to be tried because we were juveniles.

"My friends were not so lucky. The police found out that they were not citizens. They themselves had no idea! An investigation into their background showed that their parents had migrated into the United States illegally, and they still had no papers."

As Fredrick narrated his story, he had tears in his eyes.

"They were immediately deported. Patrick to Haiti and Roberto to Venezuela.

"I was lucky. Because of the addiction, I got a year of rehab. The news, however, did not go down well with my mom. Then before I could get out of rehab, she got hit by a bus and died.

I decided to start my life afresh. I took a counseling course and became a counselor for Young Persons in Rehab. Then I enrolled for college and attended night

classes. That was how I got my degree in Psychology.

"Not everyone will get lucky as I got. I do not know what happened to my friends. Have not heard from them since then. One thing I realized is that everyone has a separate path to take. But life will throw a lot of stones and bricks at you. Just make sure those things do not derail you."

Derek was surprised. Little wonder he was able to connect with him. He made a decision not to go down the same drain he'd once found himself.

They both drove back in silence.

Fredrick hoped that he had been able to fuel the young man's resolve to stay off drugs. Derek realized that he had a golden opportunity, and he was not going to let anything get in his way.

ANDERSON DOVILAS

THE FOLLOWER

My name is Jasmine. I am a regular 16-year-old girl but I have no close friends. Do not get me wrong. I am not disabled, nor retarded, nor anti-social. Neither am I loner. I get along fine with everybody in school, church...well, to the exception of Britney and her gang who I have decided to avoid in every way possible. You may think I am weird, but I have only learned that your type of friends can make you or mar you. Ever since my encounter with Britney and her crew, I decided to focus on being my own person before associating myself with anyone else. Well, I will tell you my story, then I will let you be the judge of my actions.
***

My mom is a very soft and loving woman. I have no recollection of my father; he died before I was 2 years old. So for as far back as I can remember, it has always been Mom and me. We attended church together, went grocery shopping together, and we hardly ever ate separately. That is, until she got promoted and became the manager of the chain of hardware stores where she worked. At that time, I was 12. As a result of the promotion, Mom started working

late. At first, I was lonely because I wasn't used to do things by myself. Gradually, I started to enjoy the freedom it afforded me. I used to take walks around the neighborhood, sit in the park, and read a novel every evening. It was on one of such trips to the park when I ran into Britney, Charlotte, Henrietta, and Betty. They were having a picnic. We attended the same church and school, but we were not close. That fateful day, they invited me to join them. I was happy to have company so I didn't hesitate. We chatted about general things and it was fun.

When it was six o'clock, I announced that I was leaving. They all looked at each other and burst out laughing. I was embarrassed and wondering what I had said that was so funny. Britney told me not to mind them, so I bade them goodbye and went home happy that I had made friends.

At school the next day, they saved a seat for me in the back row. I wasn't tall, so I usually sat in front. Unfortunately, they favored the back seats. I didn't want to lose my new friends so I sat with them. During class, we kept exchanging notes and making fun of the other students and our teacher. I found it odd and rude and I was uneasy. I tried hard to listen to the teacher.

During break, I had lunch with them. Charlotte,

whose mom worked as a personal shopper for celebrities, kept on talking about how badly our teachers dressed. The others were inputting in the conversation. I was not so familiar about fashion because my mom always picked my clothes. I just kept smiling as they insulted all of our teachers. The topic then went from that to the richest kids in school. I was so surprised they had this kind of information.

Soon, Britney announced that she had a huge crush on our math teacher. I was shocked, because I felt like that was an adult thing to do or to say. I had no idea how it felt to have a crush on someone. I felt only adults were allowed to do that, and afterwards they would get married. I asked her why she liked him and if she was ready to get married to him now, because I thought that naturally followed from having a crush. They all made fun of me and called me a baby. I was so embarrassed that I couldn't say anything.

After school while walking home, I asked them if they wanted to do homework and study together later on. Once again they laughed at me, and Betty called me boring and nerdy. I wondered why my comment was so funny to them. Britney told me that they were big girls and if I wanted to hang out with them, I had to make sure I behaved like a big girl.

As I turned to go home, I felt like I had been living in a cage and wanted to get out. I wanted to be a big girl. I decided to ask Britney the next day what a big girl behaved like.

At school the next day, they did not keep a seat for me like they did the previous day. I was stunned, and so I dejectedly went to my usual seat like a dog with its tail between its legs. During lunch, I couldn't find them. The week went by and they all avoided me like the plague. I was hurt, and for the first time in my life I felt rejected.

***

I finally had my chance to talk to Britney in church that Sunday. I saw her go to the restroom, so I followed her. I confronted her and asked why they'd been avoiding me all week. She just sneered and kept adjusting her dress. As she was about to step out, I held her back and pleaded passionately with her to teach me what it meant to be a big girl. She looked back, surprised, and told me to meet her at the park later that evening at seven o'clock. I told her it was too late; my mom would never allow me out at that time. She simply laughed and said, "The first step to being a big girl is never take orders from anyone," and she walked away.

All through that day, I wondered how I was going

to get out of the house. My mom noticed my restlessness and was worried. I told her all was fine. Later that evening, while Mom was working on her laptop, I managed to sneak out of the house. After thirty minutes of waiting at the park, I saw Britney casually strolling through. When she saw me, she simply waved, turned around, and went back towards her house. I was surprised because I asked for a lesson and all she gave me was a wave.

Out of sadness, I walked back home. I was so focused that I forgot my mom was home and that I had snuck out. Unfortunately for me, Mom was in the sitting room. She was surprised to see me, because she thought I was asleep in my room. She asked where I was coming from. I decided it was time to act like a true big girl. I told her I was running personal errands. She got really angry and asked me, "Since when did you start running personal errands at this time of the night?"

I replied, "Mom, you do not need to shout or tell me what to do. I am a big girl now."

She was stunned. She shouted at me to go to my room and that I was grounded. It didn't bother me, though.

The next day at school, Britney, Charlotte, Henrietta and Betty were waiting for me. I was angry at Britney for what she did to me at the park. She just smiled and told me

that it was just the first step in my training. She asked me how I got out of the house. I explained my ordeal and Charlotte said it was just the first step. She told me parents were control freaks and wanted absolute control over everyone, and it was up to us to refuse that control.

Getting back home, I had gotten all the pep talk I needed from the girls. Betty told me how she had called the Department and Children and Families (DCF) on her dad to get her freedom, and I decided that I was going to do same. The prospect of living on my own in a home without my mom to supervise me thrilled me. In fact, I was looking forward to it.

That evening, I arrived back home very late. My mom was worried. When she saw I was okay, she asked where I had been when I was supposed to be grounded. I snubbed her and went to my room. On my way, she got really angry and pulled me back. She repeated her questions and I don't know where I got the courage, but I screamed back "Why are you such a control freak? I'm sure daddy had to die to escape your control!" I had hardly finished my sentence when she slapped me. I ran to my room and called 911, just as Betty had told me to do. I told them I couldn't take the beatings anymore, that she had hit me over and over. The lies just kept spilling out of me.

When the cops showed up at our door, my face was still red from the slap. My mom was surprised and hurt that I could do such a thing. When one of the social workers talked to my mom about it, she burst into tears and explained what happened. After a while, they decided I was in no imminent danger so they left with a strict warning for my mom. The cop also gave me his number and said that I could call him anytime if I felt Mom was going to harm me in anyway.

***

The next day, while I was preparing for school, my mom came in and from her eyes, I could tell that she did not sleep and had been crying all night. She told me that she had decided to let me be and that she would keep praying for me. I was happy that she was finally letting go.

All day long in school, I was on cloud nine. My friends and I were in a world of our own. I felt liberated, but from what exactly I did not know. I was just proud of my new status as a big girl.

After classes, we hung out at the mall food court reading fashion magazines. I stopped doing homework. I started dressing in a more fashionable way and started using makeup.

After a couple of weeks, Charlotte announced that I

needed to get into detention to make sure that my school record was more suitable to my status. We set to work. Before class that day, we rolled papers up into balls. During the class, we started stoning people with those papers. Then with a straight face, we'd pretend that we had no idea what was going on. When it was my turn, as soon as I threw it, the principal walked in and caught me in the act. So I got my first detention, and I was proud of it.

That night, I heard my mom praying for me. I felt sorry for her, but back then my new-found freedom was worth more than her tears. I became a rising star among my friends. To my teachers, I was notorious. To my mom, I was her failure. I found myself doing things just because I wanted to impress my friends.

During our usual sit outs, we read an article about a popular movie star who was caught shoplifting. Henrietta, with a devilish glint in her eye, said she imagined what it would be like if she could shoplift. I was horrified, because I was brought up with the mindset that stealing gets you killed. We all dismissed the idea.

Soon I realized that because of my eagerness to please my friends and fit into the big girl status, I did ridiculously mean things to my classmates and any other unfortunate kid who just happened to walk within range. I

was starting to feel restless about this. I tried refusing some of the things I was told to do, but they had this hold on me from which I couldn't break free.

***

Later that weekend, Britney said she wanted to get some supplies, so we all went to a supermarket together. While we were shopping around, I got separated from the group. I didn't intend to buy anything, I was just looking around. By the time they were done, Britney put some items which were not on her list in my pocket. She told me that they decided that we needed to do something crazy to lighten up our day, and that I had to walk out with those items undetected.

I was scared. I asked her how I was going to get out undetected. She said she was going to pay for the items in her cart so the alarm was not going to detect what I had in my pocket. I asked why we could not do it the other way around. She said it was my turn, that they had all tried it before.

I convinced myself that if they had done it before, and had scaled through it, I was definitely going to scale through as well. As we approached the register to pay for Britney's items, I was really sweaty. The attendant kept asking me if I was okay, and I said yes. Just as we were

about to leave, the alarm beeped. I knew I was in trouble. The guard on duty came around and he demanded to search us. Britney tried to say maybe the alarm picked up something in her shopping bag that the attendant did not add. When the guard searched us, the stolen items were found in my pocket. The girls looked at me in horror. They feigned innocence. Britney even denied knowledge of those items in my pocket. I was dumbfounded.

They left and the guard handed me over to a police officer who was going to take me to the juvenile detention center. On our way, he asked me some questions. How did you get into this? Do you want to spend the rest of your life in jail when you turn 18? I said no, and I started crying. I apologized and explained that I didn't want to steal anything. I begged him to call my mom. My plea fell on deaf ears.

After a few minutes of silence, he asked me to explain how I got myself into this mess, and I explained the whole story. I guess it must have touched him, because he took me home. As soon as my mom opened the door, I ran into her arms and cried. She also broke down crying. At the same time, she thanked God that her prayers were not in vain.

When we both calmed down, Mom thanked the

officer and asked what happened. I retold my story, and she burst into tears all over again. I apologized for all my actions. I promised her I would never do anything like that again.

The officer gave me a warning; he said he was going to personally check on me, and if I seemed out of control he would personally put me in jail.

Ever since, I stopped walking with Britney and her crew. They saw me in school and tried to apologize. I forgave them, but I never went back to hanging out with them again.

ANDERSON DOVILAS

THE REPORT CARD

Prologue

Matilda walked into the teacher's room, unaware of the surprise party planned for her. As she walked in, everyone started singing, "Happy birthday to you..." Her eyes were filled with tears, and she was overwhelmed with joy. She, a reject, had now become a cornerstone. Once again she had just concluded a campaign against bullying, and it was a success. She looked back at how far she had come and felt truly blessed.

***

I grew up in a good home. My parents were loving, although my dad was a tad too strict and harsh sometimes. But all in all, I had a good background. I was a bright and happy child and a blessing to my parents. All parents around me wished for a child like me. Apart from my sweet countenance, I was also very obedient and respectful. In school, I was every teacher's delight because I was not only easy to teach, I was also very intelligent. I was a rising star.

By the end of elementary school, I received a scholarship into one of the most prestigious private

boarding schools. This was where my troubles began.

The day my scholarship letter came in the mail, my parents were so proud of me. Although I was proud of myself, I did not want to go to a boarding school. I could not imagine staying with different girls I did not know. I tried to convince my dad especially, but all my pleas fell on deaf ears. My dad was adamant that I go. He felt that opportunities like that came only once in a lifetime. He also felt that I needed the exposure and after this experience, I'd be able to live just about anywhere.

My mom, on the other hand, was scared for her baby. She did not want me to go so far away from home, yet she couldn't overturn her husband's decision. So the decision was made, and I was to go to the school. On the eve of my departure, I went to my parents' room and tried once again to plead with my dad on the issue. He shunned me and told me he knew what was best for me. That night, I went to bed with a very heavy heart.

***

On my way to the school, I tried to put on a new attitude towards the school, but I just couldn't help but feel anxious. After my parents dropped me off, I was coldly received by the house mistress. As a rule, the younger students were to be allocated in a room with an older

student. I was then assigned to a room with a girl in her final year named Tricia. Tricia was tall and slender as well as beautiful. I hoped she was going to be nice and that we could eventually bond like sisters. She barely even looked at me when I greeted her. My heart sank. I tried to settle in and make myself comfortable. As I was doing that, Tricia informed me of her limits. She told me not to cross a certain side of the room and that I was not permitted to bring in friends. I was scared, and I burst into tears. I knew I was in for the long run, but I just wanted to go home.

The routine at the school was not comfortable. The schedule not convenient; there was little or no time for recreation. All we did was work. The school was more or less a prison, and we had wardens instead of teachers. They were always hostile and glued to work.

I summoned some courage and tried to go to class. On my way to the classroom, I was stopped by the hall monitor.

"Where are you off to, Madam?" he asked. He smelled like he had been in the refuse dump for days.

"I'm on my way to the classroom, Sir," I answered, visibly shaken. I was not used to having my hall pass with me, as I knew that was what he was going to ask me for.

"Where is your hall pass?" he asked. He seemed

like he had not caught anyone all week long, and seeing this easy prey had decided to pounce.

"I'm only new here, Sir; I did not bring it with me as I was rushing from the hostel, I was late for class....." I was trying to explain to him when I was shushed by his husky voice.

"Still does not matter my dear, you will have to face the consequences. Where there are no laws, there are no offenders," he said as he detached a ticket and booked me.

I was devastated; I felt like a criminal on the first day at school. I did not mean to fall into trouble that day. Just then, a group of girls passed the hall monitor. The funny part was, he didn't stop them, and they slipped something into his hands; a twenty-dollar bill. I was astonished.

So things like this happen around here, I thought as I looked at the girls. They took notice of where I was and came over. They whispered amongst themselves as they laughed. They were probably making fun of me. As they neared me, the biggest among them hit my head.

"Are you a newbie here?" she asked as she continually hit me. The other girl ransacked my bag. After scattering my backpack and making me look untidy, they left with a look of satisfaction on their faces.

It appeared these girls ran the school; they bypassed protocols and bullied me in the hall while the hall monitor looked away. I felt defeated as I went to class. I was initially late, and going through all of this delayed me even further. I was faced with another issue: how to enter the class without being questioned. I decided to skip the class. Totally defeated, untidy, and downcast, I headed for the hostel.

***

The days rolled by, and I tried to get used to the school life. I could not avoid the bullies as they constantly picked on me. The sad part was, we were all in the same class. There was a particular moment when I tried asking a question in class, but the teacher aggressively dismissed me, and the bully squad booed me until I got to the hostel.

There was a time that they tried throwing me down the stairs, but the hostel members intervened. The incident affected me for days, both emotionally and psychologically. I became very absent-minded both in class and in the hostel. My tutor, Bella, noticed, but she couldn't care less, as she despised her job, and took no special care in her students.

The absent-mindedness went on for a long time, and so did the bullying until a certain day when I was at the

cafeteria. I was peeling oranges when the girls arrived. I knew I was going to get picked on again, and I was lost in my thoughts as I imagined what they would do.

"Ouch!" I shrieked; I had cut my wrist while imagining the bully attacks, and the cut bled profusely. A lot of people rushed over to me as I was gradually fading away. Tablecloths and towels were used to apply pressure and try to stop the bleeding, yet it kept gushing out. I fainted.

When I woke up, I noticed I was at the hospital, and the blurry figure in my presence was my mom. I tried getting out of the bed but I was too weak to do so. Just then, the doctor walked in.

"How are you feeling?" she asked. The doctor was a friendly old lady whose smile was capable of healing anyone.

I smiled and nodded my head, "At least this feels better than the hostel."

Just then, the house mistress came in. I knew she was going to tell mom about the recent occurrences in school, but I didn't care at that point. I needed mom to know how I felt in school, even if the house mistress would not paint it the right way.

"Matilda has been absent-minded recently, and even

her class teacher complained about it. There is very little we can do about that, Ma'am. I suggest she go home straight from here. Thankfully, they just finished up their exams," the house mistress said.

I felt happy, at least I was going home, to a place where I could at least rest, or so I thought. I did not know that Mom had other ideas.

"This is a spiritual problem. We have to see a pastor," she said.

Dad was out of town and couldn't be reached, so Mom made the decision to take me to a spiritual father.

Once with him, Mom explained all that had happened to me, and suggested that I be left with him and his family for three days. This way, adequate counseling and prayer sessions could go on. Mom left after a few hours, and in the evening the father called me outside to have a word with him. We discussed all that had happened and he asked me a few questions. He also asked if it was related to bullying. I paused and shed tears, explaining how I'd been treated back at the hostel. He told me it was not a spiritual case, but a psychological one, as the bullies had gotten under my skin, and the thought of them had a certain impact on my mind. He suggested that I see a psychologist.

***

Three days later, Mom came back. The father tried explaining to her that it was not a spiritual case; it was rather a mental case. To my great surprise, Mom flared up and totally disagreed with the pastor. She took me away in anger. She claimed the pastor lacked faith in God and questioned his beliefs. She kept lamenting until we got home.

As soon as we got home I rested, and after a while I stood up from the bed. Unknowingly for me, the school had already emailed my dad the results of the examinations, and I had failed just two positions above the repeating zone, and he was on his way home. He didn't know anything about what had happened and he already expected me to be home since it was the holidays, so he came home with the mindset of tongue-lashing me about the results.

As he came into the house, despite the fact that I was weak, I tried going downstairs to meet him. As I got to him and tried hugging him, he refused as he pointed to my result papers. Then he started shouting at me, asking why I couldn't have performed better. I felt bad. I needed encouragement at this stage and I was getting the opposite. Just then, Mom rushed out and started hurling words at Dad for not coming home for a long time, and the whole scene changed from me being the talking point to them having

their arguments.

***

I couldn't take any of this anymore. I decided to commit suicide, and maybe I'd be free from the hassle of this life. Without thinking twice, I opened the window of my room and jumped out. As I landed, I felt myself falling on a soft material. I had expected to fall on the hard ground and shatter my bones and rupture my spine, but none of that happened. Maybe I was dead? But no, I wasn't; I'd landed on the new neighbors' foam. They had not moved it inside as they were still clearing the room. To my surprise, I could not stand; just then, the woman from the other house came out. She was in her vehicle and she'd watched as I jumped from the window, crying. She kept shouting, "It's a miracle!" until my parents heard and came out. After narrating the whole issue, she advised my parents to always consider my happiness, and in the process, she told us that she had lost her second son. He had committed suicide. My parents were visibly touched, and they began to consider changing from that day onwards.

The woman, named Mrs. Caulcrick, cared about my development. I saw her as my godmother, and she influenced my change during middle school. I am so grateful to Mrs. Caulcrick for giving me the opportunity to

live again.

***

Epilogue

Mrs. Caulcrick was not present at my birthday party. It hurt, but she made me who I am today. I went to college and studied special education. I really want to help kids and make their feelings count. Now I'm a graduate, and I have a teaching job; it's time to start helping the kids!

THE ONE TO BE BLAMED

Prologue

As John was called to the podium to give his graduation speech as the valedictorian, I was covered with goose bumps and red with pride. This was someone on whom seven years ago we could not have actually predicted this kind of success. I had wished for God to help me change him, but I never expected this latitude of change. All of a sudden, I heard, "These would not have been achieved without my sister, Jessica." He invited me to the podium for recognition. As I walked over, we both hugged, tears of joy rolling down our cheeks, and only wished that our mom was here to witness this.

***

I am Jessica Wiggins, a medical consultant. And frankly speaking, if someone had told me I would have had it this easy in the later years of my life, I would have laughed. I never found it easy growing up with a single mother. I never knew my dad or heard anything about him, and I dared not ask; my mom wasn't approachable.

I remember one day when I did try asking Mom about Dad.

"Mom, at school, other kids speak of their dads and

moms, don't I have a dad?" I'd asked. Mom heard, but decided not to answer. As a little girl, I didn't know how to read in-between the lines, so instead, I just pulled her clothes. I guess I pulled her skirt too hard, and I could remember vividly that it came down. Mom responded with a very hard slap, and I thought it was because of my yank of the skirt. Recently, I realized there was more to it.

Mom was a strict disciplinarian. She worked at the postal mail services as a secretary, and we lived in the suburbs of New Orleans. Mom had her principles, and she didn't mind breaking sticks on your back to get you to adhere to them.

"Jess, make sure John doesn't get wet and stained, your lunch is in the microwave, just warm and bring it out. Make sure it doesn't spend more than three minutes in there, 'cause I'll find out and you know what'll happened if I do," she said as she walked out. It was a rainy day, and a very cold one at that. After turning on the microwave, I went to check up on John, my brother. Unfortunately, I ended up spending more time with him because he was the troublesome type.

"Oh Snap! I forgot the food in the microwave!" I said as I rushed to the kitchen. Luckily for me, the food was not burnt, even if it cooked more than the three minutes as

Mom had specified. I returned to the living room where John was supposed to be, but he had already gone out of the house and into the rain. This spelled trouble for me as I knew Mom would find out. I felt like giving him a hot slap, as he was already a 7-year-old. He could differentiate between right and wrong, but chose to be a spoiled brat.

As I carried him inside, he started crying uncontrollably. I was irritated because after putting me in much a mess, he cried like I was treating him unjustly. As if things couldn't get any worse, Mom came back. The drainages were blocked, and there was no way she could have passed through, so she had to turn home. Hearing the honking of her vehicle seemed like a death sentence, and I wished I could just die at that moment. John was still crying, filled with wet soil, the microwave was obviously still hot, and the door was wide open. Before she came in, I started sobbing, as I knew I was going to be punished.

She stood at the entrance, in her leather jacket and boots, and as she took the rain boots off she surveyed the house. She hung her jacket on the balcony rail to avoid dripping water. She did not say a word to us, she just went straight to the kitchen. She obviously went to check the microwave.

As she came out of the kitchen, she darted out

towards me and landed me series of hot slaps. John stood there, giggling. Mom went to him, too, and beat him, even though it was not more than a few spanks at the back of his hands. I felt cheated. Mom did not ask for any explanation, did not find out that John was the cause of all this trouble. He cried for a few moments and then slept it off. I sat in the cold living room, shedding hot tears, and thinking about how badly I've been treated.

***

Over the next months, similar routines occurred, and I was beginning to wonder if I was truly her daughter, or if she had just adopted me. These incidents affected my confidence both at home and at school. It got to a stage where, if Mom wanted to stretch her arms, I flinched and had the feeling she was coming at me, and I usually tried to seek cover. I did my best to not sit by her, for if I did, a minor act could lead to slapping.

At school, I barely had any friends, and it was not because I didn't dress well. In fact, Mom made sure we were among the most neatly dressed students at school. This was reflected in my dossier, as my teacher would make special remarks about my appearance.

"Do not let that get into your head, your grade isn't so good, so try and brush up on your math sums. You had a

C there," Mom would say. Most of the time I was fired up, as this was the highest compliment I could get from her.

When it came to my grades, my teacher had no problems with me, yet I barely answered questions in class. Not because I didn't know the answers, but because I didn't have the confidence in myself to speak.

***

Weeks rolled by, and I noticed an unusual behavior in Mom. Suddenly, the once cheerful and lively mom who always gave out orders became reserved. At first I was happy, but later I became concerned. John, who barely cared, just went about his normal routine of tidying up his room and going outside to play ball.

The thoughtless brat surely doesn't notice the change in Mom's mood, I thought as I washed the dishes. Out of my absent-mindedness, a china dish slipped out of my hands and fell. It broke and shattered into tiny pieces. I was already thinking I was in for another round of battering.

As Mom walked into the kitchen, she looked at the broken plate, looked at me, and all she said was, "Be more careful with the dishes, and sweep it up so no one gets cut."

I was surprised. I'd expected a hell of a beating, or at least a twisting of my ears, but all I got was a warning. I

noticed that Mom seemed feeble and that she didn't walk upright as she used to. I was scared to ask her what the problem was, as I didn't know what the reaction would be. I decided to forget about asking her what was wrong. Just then, the telephone rang. It was Mom's only friend, her sister. I was asked to answer.

"Hey Vanessa, how are you feeling? What did the doctor say about the chemotherapy, and when is it due to start?" my aunt asked right away.

"Hello Aunt, let me get the phone to my mom," I replied, shaken. At that time, I didn't know what the chemotherapy entailed, but I knew it wasn't good in any way. I was trembling as I gave Mom the phone, not because I was scared, but because of the state I found her in when I bent over the stool to drop the phone. She picked up the phone with great difficulty, her hands trembling, and it seemed she had difficulty in breathing.

***

That night, I could hardly sleep. The thought of chemotherapy scared me. I made up my mind to check it up at the library as the library had access to the internet. The next morning, my aunt was there very early, and as I prepared for school, she offered to drop me off.

"I'll be gone for a couple of days, just make sure

everything is order. If you want anything, be sure you can get it," Mom said, sounding really weak.

I nodded as I tried getting John ready for school, but he insisted on getting himself ready, as he didn't want to be "ruled over by me." John was a spoiled boy who always had most things his way. I decided not to cause a scene, so I left him alone.

I walked slowly to school, my legs heavy. I didn't know what I would meet when I got to the library. I could hear my heart beat fast. After many unsuccessful attempts, I finally connected to the internet. As I typed out the word "chemotherapy," my heart sank. Mom had cancer! And chemotherapy was the regular treatment she'd get before surgery.

I wept for over an hour in the library, and thought of how this could happen to me. I finally braced myself and went to class. Even if I was moody, no one noticed because no one cared. I was a moody, unfriendly, and independent person.

The last bell of the day went off and I went to John's class to look for him. I noticed that he wasn't in class. After searching around the school, I found him in the field next to the school cafeteria. He was playing and enjoying himself. It felt so great seeing him smile, but the

thought of being delayed by him sparked my head.

"Come here silly, where have you been?" I said as I moved towards him.

"None of your business, you bully. Why not just leave me alone in peace?" he replied abruptly. I was surprised that it came from John. I felt bad, didn't utter a word, and I turned away. He on the other hand did not feel any remorse, and continued playing.

I left for home without him, and even though I knew he would have a hard time finding the house, he never admitted to it.

***

I got home and sat on the sofa, when I noticed a piece of paper on the table.

"Jessica, just brace yourself for the worst. I know you must have noticed changes in me recently, and I'm dying. Now, I don't know what will happen, but always remember all I've taught you, and take good care of John. Mom."

As if the day wasn't terrible enough, I'd just received a note from Mom seeming like she had accepted defeat. I sobbed uncontrollably, missing her.

I don't think I'm ready for this. Our aunt was a career woman who travelled around the world and barely

had her own time. We did not have a dad, and we didn't have any relatives nearby. All of these thoughts came to my mind as I sobbed.

When John got back from school, I explained the whole scenario to him. He was quiet for a few minutes, and all he said was, "She'll be alright."

Our aunt came over regularly to prepare food to take to the hospital for Mom. She prepared meals for us, too. At this time, I was a teenager, and I knew a lot about being a woman, and John was no longer a kid. He could fend for himself now. There was still one problem though; we still did not get along well. He talked to me like I was his housemaid, and anything that I did or told him to do was always for my own gain or was against him.

Mom came in and out of the hospital until her surgery. After the procedure, she was a shadow of her former self. She hardly talked and she was always in her bed. She stood up with the aid of a cane and grew lean.

After two weeks of being discharged, complications arose, as the cantankerous lumps resurfaced. They were full-blown cancers and mom had to be rushed back to the hospital. I knew at that stage that anything was bound to happen, and I hoped for the best while preparing for the worst.

***

Mom gave up and died in her mid-40's. Although I felt bad, I had seen it coming. Only John cried like he was not expecting it, but that was because he never paid attention to details or to what was going on around him. At her funeral, we both cried like babies. We were among very few at the funeral: just the pastor, a few members of the church, our aunt, John, and me. I held on to the coffin when it was about to be lowered into the grave and kept screaming until I was carried away.

Life after Mom's demise was not the same. I could only appreciate her more now that she was no longer with us. She taught me how to be independent in a way that I didn't realize. Because I was used to doing it all, I developed a thick skin to rejection and rarely asked anyone for help.

***

One Saturday, as I was doing the chores, which included cleaning John's room, I called him over.

"John, can you help me with the brooms?" I asked. I had just finished with washing the dishes and John was busy doing nothing. I didn't feel any different, as Mom usually made me do all the chores at home anyway, which also included taking his bedspread out and sweeping the

room. I would also help him arrange his toys. There was a particular time I felt I was being used as his nanny, but I'd already developed resistance to that.

"Why do I need to help you? Isn't it your duty? Deal with it," he said as he turned back to his headsets. I was outraged, I rushed out to him and dragged the headsets from him, and then a fight ensued.

We pinched and hit and dragged until we were both tired. Just then, our aunt came in.

"What is the meaning of all this? You think all this would happen if your mom were here? Why would you keep fighting? Can't you live as one? Do you think your mom would be happy if she sees what's happening between you two?" she said.

The mention of mom made both of us break down. We obviously didn't know how to get along, but we had to. We had to stand for ourselves as we were all we had at this stage. We both apologized to each other.

John surprisingly changed after that. No one knew what prompted it, but I think he just turned into a man. He had stopped being a boy and learned to admit his own wrongs.

***

Days rolled into weeks, and weeks into months. The

annual scholarship offer was out and the offer was for anyone who had a cumulative GPA of 3.5 and above. I readily applied, as we were on scholarship by the post office, who had used it as a tribute to Mom for her long-serving years, and the scholarship ended at the high school level.

It still remained with me that Mom had died of cancer, and I needed to find out what could be done to prevent more casualties. I therefore decided to venture into medicine. John, on the other hand, was business inclined, and even if he was two years younger than me, he knew what he wanted at that stage.

It was time for the exams, and in the science section, we were asked to answer one question out of three. The first question came to me as a surprise: "What is chemotherapy?"

***

Epilogue

As expected, I got the scholarship thanks to the question that came my way. I couldn't thank our aunt more for the support she gave, and John for being a mature, young, and understanding man. I studied and came out with flying colors, though not the top of the class. I got a job as a consultant in the federal hospital. John was exceptional,

and I could not have been happier to have him as my brother.

THE STORM

The clouds are always dark these days. It's almost the end of spring, and it makes me sad that the best season of the year is almost over. Everyone is gladly awaiting the fun times. Well...everyone except Mr. Burke, who always thinks that there is doom lurking at every corner when students have to take a break from school. We all thought it would be business as usual; the kids would have their fun times and people would visit nice places and all that.

My best friend Nicky and I had made plans already. We would go camping. We had made preparations for several years now, but we could never really agree on the right date. We both wanted to go to someplace fun together, but each time we came up with a plan my mom could never seem to take some time to drop us off at the campsite. On most occasions she was very busy, as she was a nurse at the local hospital who loved her job and barely had time for anything else. I don't know if she made those excuses because she was busy, or because she liked to know that I was close by and that I was safe. I think the idea of being out in the field exposed to God knows what scared her as much as it excited me.

This time however, it was part of a school trip for students who were interested in nature and wildlife

photography. It was partly sponsored by the school and I had saved up money for the trip from last summer when I worked at the ice cream shop. I saved every penny and I was sure this year that I would go.

Anyway, everyone has been saying that this year has been good, so I guess the goodness would also get to me, too. Spring gave me much joy, and maybe that is also the reason why I looked forward to the summer break. Most of the other kids are not concerned about the heat; we stay outdoors and get all the fun we can before school reopens.

***

Grown-ups never seem to enjoy this period at all. Mom comes back from work complaining about the stress and the heat. My dad, Paul, is the worst. He works as a real estate agent and spends most of his time outside showing people houses. Whenever he's not at work, he spends the day in front of the television mostly talking to the TV people and then listening to them. He would make us dinner most times, and made sure we have a nice family experience.

Dad has a spooky habit of checking the door all the time to make sure it is locked after anyone comes in, although our street is usually safe and the sheriff does not

live far away. Besides, there has not been a case of any kind of attack for almost three years now, and everyone lived with a relatively good sense of security. Most nights when I cannot sleep, I go down to watch late night movies, but my dad wakes up at the slightest sound and he doesn't like to see the lights inside the house on at night because he thinks it will attract unwanted attention. He made me stop my late night TV habit, and instead I stare at the ceiling and count one to ten until I doze off. My dad still checks the windows at the slightest sound; it doesn't matter what time of the day it is.

***

When I got home, I was shocked to see that he was already home. He seemed to be in a bad mood and on edge for some reason. He gave an absent-minded reply when I said hello. I went into my room, but I heard him ranting to himself a few minutes later. I called out to him to make sure he was okay. "Isabelle, come down here!" I wondered if I had done anything wrong as I walked down the stairs. I found him standing in front of the television muttering to himself. He made me sit down and started to tell me about the things the reporter had said. He was convinced the governor was a party to some dirty schemes and said he would be exposed soon.

Nicky came over to our house, complaining that she feared her test scores in algebra would not be so good. Dad overheard our discussion as he passed the kitchen and came back to reassure her that the test scores would come out alright. True to his word, she got a B+. He asked her about it when she came visiting another day, and as she told him her scores, he looked at me knowingly and then said in a happy voice, "Told you so, didn't I?"

He was now convinced he was a prophet of some sort. He would relate to me how some ancient members of his ancestry had been known to have the gift of clairvoyance. We laughed about this on our way back from school. Dad was funny and he had a good heart, he was just sometimes surprising.

***

I was packing my clothes getting ready for camp, and we were set to leave the next day when Dad came into my room. He stood at the doorway with a look of sadness on his face. "There's a storm coming," he announced. I didn't want to be negative about the news so I replied that hopefully it would clear up before we have to leave.

"Sorry to disappoint you darling, but this storm is not going to let up anytime soon. It's on the news." I pushed past him as I ran downstairs to see the forecast. I

replayed the recording. It was true that there was a storm coming, but Dad had blown it a bit out of proportion. The forecaster said that the storm would probably last an hour.

Dad, however, insisted that the storm would go on for days. He said we had to make preparations, and he called Mom at the hospital and told her about it. He took out his debit card and went out to the store, saying he had to get provisions ahead of the storm. I went back to my room to finish my packing. I called Nicky, and she assured me that the storm would not last that long. Maybe we had disappointed my dad in not believing him, because he looked wounded as he left the house. I was sorry I could not believe him this time, but I had waited for the opportunity to go on this trip for a long time.

Hours later, I heard the sound of Dad's car as he parked outside. He began to carry in the things he had bought from the store. There were so many provisions it seemed enough to feed us for months. We arranged them in the kitchen. He also bought medical provisions for the first-aid box. I helped him arrange the bandages and other items. He bought rain boots and coats, an inflatable boat, toiletries, flashlights, canned food, bottled water, water purifier, and just about any other thing you could think of.

He was not sure Mom would come back in time to

avoid the storm, and I tried to convince him that it would not last that long so he didn't have to fear for her sake. He said he trusted Mom to take care of herself but it didn't stop him from calling her every few minutes. He went around the house, securing the doors and windows and putting things in order.

***

I left him just as he was beginning to make dinner. The clouds were already gathering and it was drizzling. I soon dozed off and was awakened by a clash of thunder that struck at my window. I had forgotten that it was still open, and I rushed to close it. I went downstairs to find my dad by the phone. He was trying contact my mom again. It had started to rain heavily by this time. Mom's cell was switched off, and this made Dad worried. He was finally able to get through to the hospital and was informed that she had already left. We waited a bit more, and I was sure that he was going out to look for her when she called to tell him that she was safe in a shelter. It was a relief to the both of us as we sat down to our meal. Hopefully, the storm would let up so I could go on my camping trip.

After dinner, I called Nicky again and we talked a bit about the storm. I told her about Dad's predictions. It worried me a bit, but she convinced me it was not going to

be the case this time. Four hours later, it seemed the storm had increased. I watched as the wind slapped the branches of trees around us. It was barely four o'clock, but the streets were already dark. Thankfully, the electricity hadn't gone out so the street lights were still on. There were flashes of lightning every few seconds followed by the boom and clapping of thunder.

In a split second, there was a loud bang and the lights went out. They came on again some seconds later, just enough for me to find my way downstairs. Dad had been watching the news, and they said the flood was rising fast. Thankfully, our house is located on the high area of the town. Those in the lowlands are not so lucky. Dad told me that some already had their roofs blown off. It had barely rained for three hours and the streets were already flooded. I was beginning to think that maybe Dad was right again this time.

The lights had been blinking as I came down, but they were off now. Dad had a flashlight with him, and he turned it on long enough for me to find my way to the sofa. He sat beside me. We sat in silence for what seemed like a decade, then Dad cleared his throat. "I hope your mom is safe wherever she is." I couldn't see his face, but I could tell he had a sad and gloomy expression. I tried to reassure

him.

"She said she found a nice shelter. I guess she's safe."

We sank back in silence before he went off to look for something. He came back with a small radio and some batteries that he had purchased in the store earlier. He turned it on and turned the dial until we found a frequency that was still broadcasting. There was a lot of talk about the flood situation in different places.

***

My dad and I were seated on the sofa, listening to the news, when there was a sudden thunder clap. Then came a flash of lightning, and the house next door seemed to go up in flames. It was Mrs. Palmer's place. Ironically, she had just recently paid off the mortgage.

Dad sprang into action immediately. We had to help them. Mrs. Palmer had three kids and they were probably all in the house. Dad put on his raincoat and boots and asked me to remain in the house while he went over to help them. The kids were crying when he got there because their mother had been hit by something and she was lying on the floor unconscious. He picked them up and carried them over one at a time. By the time he carried out their mother, other neighbors were already coming out to help. Together

they were able to put out the fire while Dad took care of the family. I fetched the first-aid kit as he patched Mrs. Palmer up. She was now awake, but still yet to recover. Once she saw that the kids were safe, she relaxed and went back to sleep, thanking Dad before she dozed off.

***

The fire couldn't be put out because the house was already engulfed in flames before the fire fighters arrived at the scene. Luckily, Mrs. Palmer was not awake to witness this. I fed the children and soon managed to put them to sleep amidst many questions about their house.

The streets were flooded by now, and Dad went back outside to help put out the fire. I turned on the radio and was informed that most of the streets on the lowlands were already flooded. I was glad to hear that the hospital was not affected. Many people were losing their homes to the flood. What surprised me most was the speed at which the flooding happened. It was just twelve o'clock, and it had been raining for about nine hours now without any sign that it was going to stop.

I was standing at the window watching the fire fighters and neighbors work when a vehicle drove past the house. It went a bit further and the engine seemed to die off. The driver climbed out and picked up the hood, trying

to revive the engine. He had a woman and a small child in the car with him. He returned to the vehicle and talked to the woman, telling her to stay in the car and he would go for help. He approached my dad, who was still helping put out the house fire, and they returned to the car and helped the child out. Dad carried her back to the house, covering her with the umbrella he had with him, and then he returned for the mother. By the time they both returned to the house, the men were drenched. I noticed that the woman was pregnant, and I brought her clean towels to dry off. The little girl was sleepy and I put her to bed with the other kids. When the fire was finally out, Dad returned home and I finally got some sleep. He made sure everyone was tucked in nicely, and I'm sure he spent some of the remaining part of the early morning thinking about Mom's safety before he dozed off on the sofa. He must have been exhausted.

***

The next morning, I was grateful that dad had stocked the house with supplies. We had almost everything we needed. It was a good thing that we had canned food and cereals, because the power and gas had gone out, and there was no running water. We used the reserve camp gas stove Dad had purchased, and he filled up some containers

with rainwater. The grown-ups made coffee on the gas stove and the kids ate cereal. To top it off, the phone lines were dead and I could not get through to Nicky or Mom.

With every meal, the four kids and three grown-ups ate together. Dad didn't ration the food or have any restrictions because no one knew how long the storm would last. Mrs. Palmer had regained herself, even though she was distraught and homeless for the time-being. Mr. Richard and his family were doing fine. They had been hoping to get to a motel before their vehicle broke down.

***

Since the rain had not stopped yet, Dad said that they were all welcome to stay until the floods cleared. It was already three days and it was still raining. At the rate we were going, the stock of food we had would be exhausted soon. Dad insisted that the kids would be fed a full portion anyway and kept as happy as possible.

I was curious. Why would he take in these total strangers and help them this much? Richard only wanted to borrow a tool to fix his car, but instead Dad took him in. And Mrs. Palmer, she hardly talked to anyone in the neighborhood, except Polly, who everyone talked to because she was a busybody who just could not be avoided. I cornered him when he was alone in the kitchen watching

the rain. I heard the crash of a falling tree as I walked in and I jumped, startled, but I soon recovered.

Dad answered my question, "The life we have in this world is meant to be shared with others. There is no joy in hoarding what you have when others need it. You only find fulfillment in sharing and caring. I took these people in because I knew it was the right thing to do. If providing them food and shelter would help save a life, then I will not deny anyone.

"Sometimes we have to learn how to eat to survive. The world is not just made for certain people, but for all people. Dream to feel alive, and love as though it was the one last best thing to do."

***

I don't think I will ever forget these words, just as I will never forget the storm. I was glad for the lessons I learned. When the storm was finally over, Mrs. Palmer began to associate more with the neighbors. We found out that she wasn't such a snob after all. Richard and his family sent us postcards and pictures from their travels and even the picture of their new baby.

SEALED LIPS

It was Friday again, and the taxi had just dropped the boy at his father's place. His mom had been too busy to pick him up, and his dad had always been busy from the day he was born and for all of his ten years on earth. He has had to live knowing he was a product of circumstance, a mere disturbance, but it was okay. He had come to terms with his position, but there was nothing else he dreaded more than walking into the imposing building before him. He had begged his mother to allow him stay back many times, but she'd refused. It did not matter if he pretended to be sick; the trick did not work anymore. She still bundled him off every Friday to his father's house.

He slowly walked toward the house and pressed the bell. A minute later, a beautiful lady opened the door. The woman was Martha, his father's wife. She had the air of a wealthy woman around her, the kind that people wore when they are held in high esteem, and it was well deserved as she was indeed wealthy on her own. It helped too that she was married to a wealthy and powerful man. She was aware that almost every woman envied her. From her looks, you could tell that she had excellent taste and a love for quality. She stepped aside to let the boy in with a cute smile on her face. The boy walked into the house and as

she closed the door behind him, she stooped down in a squat and gave him a long hug, and then kissed him on the forehead. It was such a lovely replica of a mother and son embrace that the scene would make anyone who did not have a child cry. Except that she was not his mother, and she had started kissing him on the lips.

She stopped after a minute and stood up. She asked him to take his bag into his room and come down for lunch, which he did. She had prepared a lovely meal. Once the boy sat at the table she passed him a plate but she would not let him eat in peace. This made him pick at his food and stare into the plate like he was trying to uncover some deep mystery. She continued to hover around him for a while, then she finally left him, chuckling to herself and calling him "naughty." The boy continued to pick at the food, and once the lady left he started to eat in a hurry. Whenever Martha came back in, he resumed his former attitude.

Once he was done with the meal, he went into his room and locked himself in. He began to play an electronic game, but it wasn't long before a voice rang out calling out his name, "Joshua!" He quickly lay back on the bed pretending to be asleep. She came stomping on the stairs and knocked on the door. She continued to knock until he could no longer pretend. He got up and opened the door.

She came into the room and chastised him for not answering and then asked him why. He explained that he had been asleep. She then sat on his bed and began touching his hair. She kissed him on his forehead and began to kiss him all over. She got off the bed and pulled him by the hand into her room, then she lay there on the bed with her legs apart. He knew what he was expected to do, but he didn't want to. He just sat there without moving.

She had come to accept that she could not always bully him for fear that he would tell his mother what they were doing. But she was convinced that, for some reason, he might refrain from telling her when he did try to say something. He was a quiet child and easily overlooked, and she knew how to manipulate. Although he had threatened several times before that he would tell his mother, he had never really gotten to doing it.

"Josh darling, you don't want me angry now do you? I can tell your father how much of a naughty boy you have been. I wonder what he will say to you. Or your mother, do you think she will be pleased to hear all the things I will tell her? You will be grounded for months if we are not careful."

Joshua was almost in tears and as much as he

endured his father's neglect, he couldn't bear to see the look of disappointment on his face on his account. He gradually edged toward the woman and buried his face in between her thighs as she told him what she wanted.

When he was done with his duties, she encouraged him to take off his trousers and put his penis into her. He obeyed, as always, until she had gotten all the pleasure she wanted. Afterwards, she made him lie down beside her and she began to tell him how bad he was. "All men are evil," she said, "They make you love them, then they'll hurt you or leave you.

"You will soon join them, miserable beasts," she hissed. He received similar lectures almost every time. He wondered how males could be so wicked. He did not want to anger her further because he did not want her telling his father bad things about him. He knew that adults hardly believed children.

***

Joshua knew he had to tell his mother. She scolded him for touching his zizi when she entered into his room and caught him playing with himself. This was barely two years ago. He was 8-years old then but the memory was still fresh in his mind. If his mother had thought it wrong that he was playing with his body, then she would probably

consider it worse that someone else was touching him. Martha had told him to keep what she termed their "fun secret" between them alone. This, more than anything, convinced him it was wrong for her to touch him in the ways that she did.

***

He had packed his bags to go home. He had never liked visiting his father, but Mother said it is what must be done. He was waiting for his father's return so he could go back home. Martha came into his room again. As was her habit, she did not knock. She had a package of cupcakes that she said was for his mother. She sat on the bad and as usual reached for him. He shrank away. He did not want her touching him again. It was painful with every move away from her. She kept coming closer until he got up from the bed and made to leave.

She started crying telling him that he reminded her so much of his father and all she wanted was to love him. She said there was no better way to express this than in the way she did. She walked up to him and began to kiss him again, caressing his face. This time, he did not try to avoid her. He was grateful when the doorbell rang. It was his mother. She had come to pick him up today, which was unusual. Joshua had never been happier to see her. He

quickly took his already packed suitcase back into the car where he sat waiting for his mother. She and Martha were exchanging pleasantries, and Mother was concerned with his behavior but his stepmother was very reassuring that he had been a good boy.

***

On their way home, it was clear that he was bothered for some reason and he looked saddened and deep in thought. Mother asked him what the problem was, and he began to tell her of the things Martha did to him whenever he went on those weekend trips to visit his dad. He begged her to not force him back to the house again.

His mother listened to him intently and he was almost convinced that she believed him and began to feel a wave of relief for having told her. Then she began to scold him. She accused him of trying to avoid seeing his father. "That is very insensitive of you Josh. I love you, but you know I need some time to myself too. You have to spend time with your father. We have talked about this before. He loves you but just does not know how to be a father."

"I am not trying to avoid visiting him. I just told you it doesn't feel right the way Martha touches me," he replied in frustration. How could it be that his mom didn't understand? Could it be he had read her wrong?

"And to think that you would accuse the lovely lady of such a preposterous act does not portray responsibility in any way." She continued saying that all he had said made little sense to her. She was always distracted by people she considered incapable of shortcomings.

She was admonishing him that it was wrong to lie. She reminded him of that time when he had broken grandma's favorite vase and had kept mute about it and everyone thought it was his cousin Francis who did it, until Betty told them she had seen him when he tripped and fell, accidentally breaking the vase in the process. Mom had been pissed at him that he initially denied it was his fault, and had ever since threw it in his face whenever she wanted to correct him on something. The poor boy could not stand being called a liar. This time he was saying the truth. The tears welled up in his eyes and he tried very much not to cry, but they soon ran down his cheeks of their own free will.

On seeing the tears, Mother became even more furious. She slapped her hands against the steering wheel. "Stop crying for Christ sake. You are no longer a baby!" Then in a voice that did not sound like hers, she told him to be responsible and stop playing around. This did not stop the tears as he continued to sulk.

He had learned his lesson. He promised not to tell Mother such things anymore. When they got back to the house, he ran into his room. He could hear his mother telling someone over the phone about it and he knew it would be Grandma. He wet his pillow with all the tears, but it made no difference. The next week, he'd be bundled off again to his father's house where Martha could fiddle with him and rape him as many times as she wished. He had come to terms with the experience. She told him that the experience was pleasurable, but he was still trying to understand how all this pain he felt could be seen as pleasure. He felt a terrible ache in his heart whenever she came into his room or called him into hers. There was also this terrible sense of guilt that overwhelmed him. He had made a promise to himself a long time ago that he would no longer cry.

It was the trend that once father was out of the house she would reach for him. His father was an unconsciously unconcerned man whom they both loved. Maybe that is why Martha had concluded that having him do the things his father had failed to do would be a form of compensation. He had been merely 6-years old when she started using him for her own pleasures, and he had come to accept it with the passing of time.

The entrance door burst open and Mom came in. She stood there, shocked, as Joshua continued to eat. He did not move even though he had looked up and saw her standing there. She had forgotten her flash drive in the kitchen. She had intended to use the doorbell, but for some reason decided to try the door handle and it was unlocked.

Martha could not believe her ill luck. She jumped up at the sound of the door opening; she had never been careless in leaving the door open before. Now she had the one person who she should not have seen staring at her in shock. She felt a wave of sickening horror at knowing that her well-decorated reputation would be shattered. She thought fast, "This is not what you think Sarah, it is much more complex."

"Oh really, how complex?" asked his mother, now sneering.

"Look, your son saw something he should not have seen, so he blackmailed me into providing sexual relief for him. You know he is just a young boy and they like to experiment. He probably has a crush on me or something. I tried to tell you, but I just didn't know how to go about it."

One did not need an interpreter to tell that Mother was not buying her lies. She was clearly furious now. She charged at Martha, but must have remembered something,

and instead turned to look toward Joshua. "Get your things. Let's go home," she said.

***

In the car, they drove in silence for awhile when she parked and asked him why he had not said anything about what was happening to him in the house. She stared hard at him as though she wanted, for a split second, to believe Martha's fabricated version of the story. He reminded her of all the times he had tried to tell her, especially when he had plainly told her when the abuse had started. His mother then began to cry. She reached out to hug him, but he pulled away within the limited space of the vehicle. It was not much, but it clearly showed that he was not in need of any form of affection from her. She then started the car and cried all the way home.

She was the most sorry he had ever seen her. He did not feel bad or sorry for himself; in fact he did not know if he felt anything but a deep sense of emptiness. He also felt relieved that he had finally been vindicated. Mother had come to see that he was not a liar after all. She had apologized to him over and again, but he did not seem to notice. He had harbored resentments against her for a long time because she had not believed him. Now, he did not know what to do with all those feelings.

His mother cajoled him into seeing a psychologist, which he did. True enough, he was getting help, but he was also more sensitive. Mother began to realize that it was possible that other mothers were allowing their children to suffer through this kind of abuse without knowing because they held some people in high esteem, or because they just did not believe or trust their children enough. For this reason she began an online campaign with the aim of enlightening other mothers. Joshua was also very willing to share his experience and with their joint effort, other mothers began to speak up about their ignorance. They began to educate parents on the possibility of abuse on their children by anybody. They also set up a foundation aimed at educating both parents and their children against abuse. One of the major sponsors of the foundation is Joshua's father. He was sorry he had exposed the boy to such a troubled childhood, and was desperately trying to do anything to set it right. Of course, Martha was already serving her jail sentence. The police were able to dig up evidence of other forms of prying on children; it seemed Joshua was not her only victim. His mother's testimony ensured that she was locked behind bars for a long time. It is of little wonder, therefore, that the campaign was tagged, "Listen; one pervert down, many more to go."

PARADISE PLACE

ABOUT THE AUTHOR

Anderson Dovilas was born in Port-au-Prince on July 2, 1985 and grew up in Mirebalais, Haiti, the city where his parents were born. There he went to Jean Phillipe Daut Elementary School. Later, he attended Lycée Antenor Firmin High School and Catherine Flon High School. He went on to study linguistics and psychology at the State University of Haiti. Today, he is working on a double degree, a Master in International Community Development and a Doctorate in Philosophy and Diplomacy at Corner Stone University of Florida.

He lost his mother at the age of 15 after a terrible car accident in Port-au-Prince on February 26, 2001.

At the age of 16 he founded AJHEIN (Association of Haitian Youth for the Blossoming of New Ideas) to encourage and engage the youth in cultural and literary activities.

Just one year later, his father would pass away due to kidney failure. Anderson subsequently assumed responsibility of his two younger brothers. Today, one is a physician, and the youngest is working for his ministry.

Six months after his father's death, he joined the cultural association ZETOPACH to continue with theater

and make social progress in Haiti. Together, they have set up a scholarship that has enabled many young people to benefit from free schooling.

In 2005, Anderson also founded "All for Haiti," a group of young poetry readers from the Bethany Adventist Church, to influence other youths through committed poems to read on stage regularly. In 2006, he then joined the creation studio Marcel Gilbert, of the Justin Lherisson Library in Port-au-Prince to perfect his art.

He is also a founding member of the Society of Creole-speaking Poets, who aim to play an important role in restoring the creative imagination of many young contemporary poets, especially after the 2010 earthquake in Haiti. In a movement called "Public Stage," this circle of poets will take poetry reading to the street, to the market, and to other public space that was not originally intended to feature poets. Today, many artists, poets, comedians, and writers from this movement shine in Haitian literature.

Additionally, Anderson is a founding member of SUMEV, the first and most organized structure in the whole country after the earthquake. It was initially a regional association, but then became a national movement because of its vision.

He is a committed poet and a very prolific author in

the Haitian literature with nine published books. Even without listing literary prizes won for the glory of Haiti and his many travels to represent Haiti abroad, Anderson Dovilas honors his country wherever he goes.

BOOK PUBLISHED

a) **Pwèl nan Zo,** *poetry in Creole.* Published in *Montreal,* January 2009. *Lagomatik Publishing Company.*

b) **Les Iles en Accent Aigu,** *poetry in French* Published in *Paris,* November 2009. *Le Chasseur Abstrait Editeur Publishing Company.*

c) **Liminasyon,** *poetry in Creole.* Published in *Santo-Domingo,* May 2010. *Lafont* Publishing Company.

d) **Vingt Poème pour traverser la nuit,** *Poetry in French.* Published in *Paris,* Avril 2011. *Edilivre* Publishing Company.

e) **Laviwonn,** *poetry in Creole.* Published in *West Palm Beach,* March 2012, *Perles des Antilles* Publishing Company.

f) **Mon pays, rien de luxe,** *poetry in French.* Published in Connecticut, June 2012. *Trouvailles* Publishing Company.

g) **The Shadow of the veins,** *poetry in English.* Published in *Philadelphia,* January 2013 *Publish America* Publishing Company.

h) **BESE TRIYE,** Poetry in Haitian Creole. Published in *Leogane* in 2015 *Edition Ruptures.*

i) *Mémoire d'outre-monde,* Poetry in French. Published in *Paris* in 2015 *Edition L'Harmattan.*

ANDERSON DOVILAS

CMS
Book Publishing
6100 Lake Ellenor Dr, suite 205
Orlando, Florida-32809

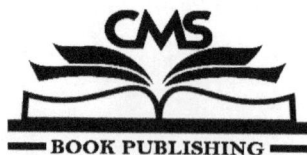

www.ingramcontent.com/pod-product-compliance
Lightning Source LLC
Chambersburg PA
CBHW021242090426
42740CB00006B/655